GRACE

GRACE

Knowing His Favor,
Gaining His Strength

STEVE HANKINS

Grace—
Knowing His Favor, Gaining His Strength

This Edition: 2021

ISBN: 978-1-7373836-0-4

Design and Typesetting by Great Writing Publications
www.greatwriting.org
Taylors, SC, USA

IS20210618

To

my wife Sandy,
with love and
"honor as a fellow heir
of the grace of life."

1 Peter 3:7

And my sons and daughters

Stephanie, Dean, Stephen, Sherilyn, Eric,
Samuel, and Viviana

3 John 1:4

Table of Contents

Preface

Like many believers, I was introduced to the idea of God's grace from Ephesians 2:8–9, "For by grace you have been saved through faith; and that not of yourselves, it is the gift of God." As a seventeen-year-old rebel against all things godly and good, God opened my eyes to the gift of salvation He was giving me through Christ's grace, while lying in a bunk bed during a late-night prayer meeting at a Christian camp. I had decided to go on that week of "vacation" at the last minute, when encouraged by my mother. That was spiritually shrewd encouragement from a mom who knew the desperate spiritual needs of her only son, who had long heard the truth but was rejecting it. Suddenly, lying in the darkness that night, while a room full of other teenage guys were praying, the light of the gospel of Christ shown into my heart. My resistance to Him melted; I yielded myself to Jesus as my Lord and Savior. I was saved by His grace.

From that moment forward, everything changed. I had ignored the Bible, now I could not get enough of it. I thought Christian music was tedious and boring, now all I wanted to listen to was *that* music, psalms, hymns and spiritual songs. To me, before that night, Christians were, well, just weird and uninteresting. Now, they were the ones I wanted to be around and develop friendships with. God and godliness had been things to avoid but now they became my passion. Sin had been my life. Now it was the thing I most wanted to avoid and proved the greatest hindrance to my new walk with God. I often felt completely powerless to overcome its power in me. I began to realize that the same favor and power from God that had made me a child of God and rescued me from eternal hell (His grace), was something I needed every day to be delivered from sin and kept in the narrow way of His will. "The gospel of the grace of God" was my only hope for success in this life-long journey I was facing.

As life unfolded—university, seminary, marriage, and ministry—I was constantly faced with my many weaknesses spiritually and my desperate need for His favor and strength—His grace. At one especially critical crisis point of spiritual warfare and extreme ministry overcommitment, I launched into a desperate search through all the passages in Scripture that mentioned anything about receiving strength or power from God. This led me, in time, to 2 Corinthians 12:7–10, which unlocked the treasure room of understanding I had needed about the grace of God, what it really is to know His favor and gain His strength, daily.

Coming to this clearer understanding of the grace of God naturally resulted in a desire to teach and preach about it to other Christians. Finding riches in the Word of God like this great truth is compelling. Sermons preached on the subject followed, in various iterations over the years. Later, brief Christian magazine articles were penned and published on the topic. Next, the writing of a short book on the subject became more than a passing thought; it became a persistent urging, a responsibility consistently presenting itself to me. Believers understand this faithful ministry of the Spirit of God in their hearts. The only right response is to obey, doing the righteous thing you are being urged to do, assuming that "urging" is consistent with the teaching of the Scriptures. Following that direction from God, I have learned anew that Christ's grace truly is amazing! It is beyond all that we could ever ask or think. I hope that same amazement captures your heart as you read what follows.

Steve Hankins
Greenville, SC
June 21, 2021

Amazing Grace

Amazing grace how sweet the sound
That saved a wretch like me
I once was lost but now am found
Was blind but now I see."

Was grace that taught my heart to fear
And grace, my fears relieved
How precious did that grace appear
The hour I first believed.

Through many dangers, toils, and snares
We have already come
T'was grace that brought us safe thus far
And grace will lead us home.

When we've been there ten thousand years,
Bright shining as the sun,
We've no less days to sing God's praise
Than when we first begun.

John Newton, 1725–1807
Slave ship captain, later a Christian, pastor, aboli-
tionist, and spiritual mentor to William Wilberforce,
Member of the British Parliament, who led in the
abolition of slavery in the British Empire in 1833.

Key Texts on Grace

"For by grace you have been saved through faith; and that not of yourselves, it is the gift of God; not as a result of works, so that no one may boast. For we are His workmanship, created in Christ Jesus for good works, which God prepared beforehand so that we would walk in them."
Ephesians 2:8–10

"And God is able to make all grace abound to you, so that always having all sufficiency in everything, you may have an abundance for every good deed."
2 Corinthians 9:8

"And He has said to me, 'My grace is sufficient for you, for power is perfected in weakness.' Most gladly therefore, I will rather boast about my weaknesses, so that the power of Christ may dwell in me."
2 Corinthians 12:9–10

"But I do not consider my life of any account as dear to myself, so that I may finish my course and the ministry which I received from the Lord Jesus, to testify solemnly of the gospel of the grace of God."
Acts 20:24

1

A Right Starting Point for Understanding

When you want to understand a major truth for Christian living, a good place to begin is the nature of God Himself. The New Testament describes Christ as "being full of grace and truth" and that from Him we will receive "grace upon grace" (John 1:14,16). The writer to the Hebrews calls the Holy Spirit the *"Spirit of Grace"* (Heb 13:9), describing Him as characterized by this divine quality. And in a sweeping encouragement to believers, Peter, the leader of the twelve apostles, wrote that *"the God of all grace*, who called you to His eternal glory in Christ Jesus, will himself perfect, confirm, strengthen, and establish you" (1 Pet 5:10).

Each of these statements reflects a frequently repeated description of God in the Old Testament, that He is "compassionate, *gracious*, slow to anger, and abounding in lovingkindness" (Ps 103:8 et al). God is by His very nature determined to show us undeserved, unearned favor as a gift. As the well-known statement of Paul in Ephesians 2:8–9 says, "By *grace are you saved* through faith, that not of yourselves, it is the gift of God; not as a result of works, so that no one may boast." In addition, God is always willing to cause each believer's "heart to be *strengthened by grace*" (Heb 13:9) day by day, so that we may *"have grace*, by which we may offer to God an acceptable service with reverence and awe" (Heb 12:28).

As the New Testament unfolds this essential theme for us, you will see that the title of the famous hymn "Amazing Grace," written by John Newton, a former slave ship captain who later became a pastor, author, and hymnwriter, is the only right way to describe this divine quality. It truly is amazing! *It is God's undeserved favor extended to all Christians in power to save them and strengthen them for Christian living.* So, let's explore the ways Christ shows us this undeserved favor to both strengthen us spiritually, and also how we can daily access all the grace from God we need as believers. I want to show how this theological truth intersects daily Christian experience, so there will at times be an intentional, autobiographical flavor to what follows.

Questions for Reflection and Discussion

1. *What is a good place to begin in seeking to understand any major truth for Christian living?*

2. *Which is the idea most opposite the Biblical idea of grace?*

3. *Which member(s) of the Trinity is (are) described as characterized by grace?*

4. *On the basis of whose work will the believer receive grace from God?*

5. *How does the New Testament describe the amount of God's grace available to the Christian?*

2

Saved by Grace

I remember as if it were yesterday arriving at the Christian university I attended for undergraduate studies. I had been a Christian for barely one year. I had left my "war torn" home behind. Mom had become a believer in Christ at a large city-wide evangelistic crusade that was held in the capital city of our state. She drove an hour one way to that crusade each night with a friend, and before the crusade week was over, Christ had found her, a lost sheep that He claimed for His glory. She was totally transformed.

But Dad was a hard-driving businessman, a nominal Christian, who was determined to achieve one thing in life primarily—the accumulation wealth. It didn't make for a happy home. Mom's and Dad's goals were now polar opposites, adding to their already polar opposite dispositions and personalities. Mom's goal was to serve Christ and be like Him. Dad's was to gather all the money he could, as fast as he could, to become as rich as he could. He was austere, frugal, and driven, and of course, I loved and admired him as his only son.

Finally, they separated during my senior year in high school, a terribly hard thing for my mother who was a relatively new Christian. Mom moved to Florida with my younger sister, and Dad remained behind with me "so I could finish my senior year in high school." It was a thinly veiled cover story that allowed them to get away from each other, without admitting directly to their children that their marriage was failing. Actually, being apart *did* help their marriage relationship, which continued until my dad's death in January 2017 at age 89, after 68 years of marriage! During that crisis year of marital separation, Dad trusted Christ as his Savior through the ministry of a faithful pastor, and things began to change for the better in our family. Eventually, all my siblings and I would at some point in our lives enter full-time, vocational Christian service. In his older years, Dad served as a deacon in a gospel-centered, Bible-believing church. Today, our extended family, though not sinless of course or free from failure in walking with Christ at times, experiences wonderful Christian unity and love for each other. We are believers at various levels of maturity, as are our children and our grandchildren, except for those who are still too young to understand the gospel. And we are praying for them and leading them to the Savior, for His glory. God works miracles in families by His grace. Our family is proof of that!

During my last year of high school, though now a Christian, I struggled with sinful habits that I had added to my life over five years as a teenager, but I had made a basic life-transforming decision at a Christian camp in the summer before my senior year, which my mother had gently and wisely suggested I attend, "just to have a nice week of vacation on an island in Lake Erie," the Great Lake our northern Ohio city sat on. I decided to go because I knew there would be some good times boating, water skiing, and swimming. I also knew there would be some new, "cute" girls I could get to know. Yep, those were my "deeply spiritual" motivations as a lost teenage guy for going to a Christian camp that week. Thankfully, God uses the foolishness of man to praise Him and work out His good providence in the lives of lost ones, like me.

Camp Patmos was named after the famous island of exile in the Aegean Sea, forty miles off the coast of Greece, where John the Apostle wrote the Book of the Revelation and saw his own glorious vision of Christ his Savior (Revelation 1:12–20). There at Camp Patmos, my eyes were opened to the truth of the gospel and I trusted Christ as my Savior and my Lord. I understood He bore my sins in His body on the cross and my punishment for them. I believed He was alive through His resurrection, conquering sin and death. I gladly accepted the gift of eternal life from Him. From that moment forward, I was resolved to follow Christ as a true disciple. In that small Christian camp on a small island during a revival among Christian teenagers, I became a different person. My basic life orientation and purpose changed instantly. I was quite literally "born again" (John 3:3). The reality of the *saving grace* of God flooded into my life. As quoted earlier in the first chapter, "By *grace are you saved* through faith, that not of yourselves, it is the gift of God; not as a result of works, so that no one may boast" (Eph 2:8–9). I had faith in Christ and this was my first taste of *grace*, His *saving grace*. Through that grace He showed His *great favor* toward me combined with His *great power* to transform me. In an instant, He gave me a new, eternal life, a relationship with God through Christ.

Questions for Reflection and Discussion

1. *What effect does a Christian in a family
    have on the other family members
    coming to know Christ's grace for
    salvation?*

2. *What effect does disharmony in a family
    have on family members coming to
    know Christ's grace for salvation?*

3. *What is a common name given to the
    grace of God resulting in salvation
    through Christ?*

4. *What is the essential response of a
    person to the good news of God's
    saving grace through Christ's death for
    sin on the cross and His resurrection, to
    be saved from sin and hell and receive
    the gift of eternal life?*

5. *What two great qualities of God are
    demonstrated by Him through his
    saving grace?*

3

Growth by Grace

When I returned home from Camp Patmos where I had come to know Christ, who is "full of *grace and truth*" (John 1:14), I gave the gospel to all my non-Christian friends in the large public high school I attended. Some of them became believers and are faithful Christians to this day. I read my Bible. I prayed. I memorized Scripture. Nobody was requiring this of me. I was hungering and thirsting after righteousness. I led a Bible study in my senior year at school and wrote articles about Christ in the school newspaper, a public high school with 2500 students. It was a great opportunity to let the Light of Christ shine into a dark place. I really believed I was His representative to others there, and that's why I gave the gospel of the grace of Christ to everybody at school, at every opportunity possible.

But when I arrived on the campus of the Christian university I was convinced God wanted me to attend at the end of the summer after high school graduation, I had not read the New Testament through fully one time, being a new believer, let alone the Old Testament, even though my heart was ablaze with love for Christ. He had saved me by His grace. Not only had He saved me from sin and eternal condemnation in Hell, He was delivering me from my sinful habits, day by day. I was "growing in the *grace* and *knowledge* of the Lord Jesus Christ" (II Pet 3:18). He was transforming me by His grace into His image, step by step. I was experiencing 2 Corinthians 3:17–18: "Now the Lord is the Spirit, and where the Spirit of the Lord is, there is liberty. But we all, with unveiled face, beholding as in a mirror the glory of the Lord, are being transformed into the same image from glory to glory, just as from the Lord, the Spirit."

His gracious *favor* and His gracious *power* were making me a new person, with new desires, new motivations, and an entirely new direction in life. He was making me like Himself, by *His grace*.

Questions for Reflection and Discussion

1. *What compelling reality will lead a new Christian to give others the gospel of saving grace?*

2. *Having experienced saving grace, how much knowledge of the Bible must the new believer have to give the gospel of Christ to others?*

3. *Though a new believer in Christ has experienced saving grace from sin and hell, what may still be true concerning his relationship to sin?*

4. *In addition to the gifts of deliverance from hell and the gift of eternal life, what begins for a new believer at the moment of saving grace?*

5. *Based on the teaching of the New Testament, what is one of the ways daily deliverance from sinful attitudes and actions is described?*

4

Gifted by Grace

Somehow, after I became a Christian that night at Camp Patmos, and before I arrived at the Christian university I had chosen to attend, I understood that my whole life, all of it, was supposed to be given over to Christ's service as a pastor, or evangelist, or in some other role in which all I would do was spread the gospel and teach others how to live for Christ. I really didn't have a clue *how* God was making me so confident about this; I just knew it was what I was supposed to do. Later I would learn that He had bestowed ministry gifts on me *by His grace* and was leading me by His Holy Spirit into the ministry.

But only after a few years of teaching from godly professors and pastors and after some Christian ministry experience did I understand the true *grace for ministry* that had been shown me by Christ. This is what the Lord Jesus does for some Christian men who will serve as church leaders and for all believers who are called to serve in the body of Christ. I was beginning to experience 1 Peter 4:10–11, which explains, "As each one has received a special gift, employ it in serving one another as good stewards of the *manifold grace of God.* Whoever speaks is to do so as one who is speaking the utterances of God; whoever serves is to do so as one who is serving by the strength which God supplies; so that in all things God may be glorified through Jesus Christ, to whom belongs the glory and dominion forever and ever. Amen."

Christ shows *His favor* by imparting *His power*

to men He chooses to speak for Him and to serve
Him in other ways, as pastor-teachers, evangelists,
missionaries, and in other roles in Christian organi-
zations. He shows that same favor and imparts that
same power to women He chooses to serve in ministry leadership positions to other women, children,
and important support roles in Christian churches,
missions and parachurch ministries. He also imparts this grace for service to *every believer*, to serve
through their spiritual gifts by grace in the body of
Christ, the church.

Questions for Reflection and Discussion

1. *What are the three great gifts given to the believer by God at the moment of saving grace through faith in the gospel of Christ, as discussed before this chapter in this book?*

2. *What is the additional blessing believers are granted at the moment of saving grace discussed in this chapter?*

3. *According to 1 Peter 4:10–11, what are the two major categories of gifts for service presented by the Apostle?*

4. *What is the basis for the gifts of service for believers given by God?*

5. *On the basis of gifts of grace for service given to each believer in the New Testament, which are the more important gifts in the body of Christ?*

5

Grace for Learning

L ife as a student at in a Christian university soon revealed to me that though I was certain I was called by God to a life of ministry for Him, I certainly was not yet qualified for such a ministry, at least not in the sense of a full-time leadership role in the church over the people of God. I was young in years and very young in the Lord. Simply put, I was an immature Christian. I needed to grow up in my walk with Christ, in character, in disposition, and in behavior. Further, there were many ministry skills I needed to add to my "set of tools" for service. What tools I did have through His gifting by grace were underdeveloped and were handled in a clumsy way spiritually as I attempted to serve.

Essential Humility

As is true of many young men called to be a disciple of Jesus, my zeal made me over-confident and, unfortunately, overbearing at times with others. I look back now with embarrassment at some of the things I did and said for "the glory of Christ" in those days as a young believer, while attempting to walk the narrow way with Him. Through failure and forgiveness, though, Christ taught me a valuable lesson I have tried to live by since. That lesson is found in two passages in the New Testament, both of which quote Proverbs 3:34. One of them is James 4:6–10: "But He gives a greater grace. Therefore it says, 'God is opposed to the proud but gives grace to the humble.' Submit therefore to God. Resist the devil and he will flee from you. Draw near to God and He will draw near to you. Cleanse your hands, you sinners, and purify your hearts, you double-minded. Be miserable and mourn and weep; let your laughter be turned into mourning and your joy to gloom. Humble yourselves in the presence of the Lord and He will exalt you."

This passage makes clear that the spiritual humility which (1) deeply and genuinely admits and confesses sins of both heart and action, (2) submits to the Lord in obedient repentance, and (3) resists Satan and his temptations will receive the grace from God needed to walk with Christ. That Christian will know the *favor of God* combined with the *strength from God* necessary to be a true disciple of Jesus, which describes the grace-filled life. In due time, the Lord will "exalt" that disciple, meaning magnify his influence with others so that he is able to serve with effectiveness as an example of Christlikeness to others for God's glory.

Quoting the same passage from Proverbs 3:34, Peter unfolds another dimension of the humility essential to receive the grace of God, *His favor combined with His strength*, to serve others for His glory. He writes in 1 Peter 5:5, "You younger men, likewise, be subject to your elders; and all of you, clothe yourselves with humility toward one another, for 'God is opposed to the proud but gives grace to the humble.' Therefore humble yourselves under the mighty hand of God, that he may exalt you at the proper time. Casting all your anxiety on Him, because He cares for you."

Young men and women called by God to discipleship may excel much older believers in zeal, obedience, and full-hearted devotion to Christ for a variety of reasons. While to love God and others with all our heart, soul, mind, and strength is precisely what we all strive for as disciples, this may become a problem, especially if younger disciples fail to understand the essential nature of submission to older leaders and teachers to assist them in their development for ministry. Many tragic failures and even ministry "shipwrecks" by younger men and women have occurred due to the neglect and even hardheartedness toward instruction from those who have proven themselves as "elders" in the Body of Christ, understood in the broadest sense of the term, rather than a formal sense.

If you are a younger person eager to serve Christ, consider that an elder is simply a mature believer. The elder may be teaching you in ministry training on the university or seminary level, or serving as your mentor-pastor in a church where you are serving during your ministry training, or he (or she) may be simply a godly, spiritually mature lay person who sets a great example of what a believer ought to be. The elder may be instructing you in the classroom, preaching to you in chapel, or serving you as a mentor or supervisor in one of the residence halls at the college or university you attend.

There is only one right response to spiritual elders God brings into your life. "Clothe" yourself in humility toward them, watch them, listen to them, and be patient. You must figuratively wrap yourself up in a genuinely humble disposition, appearance, and behavior toward them. This is like putting on a full-length coat, all buttoned up, on a cold day. A failure to do this will be manifested by the "proud look" Solomon warned about as something God hates (Prov 6:17). It may show itself by being obsessed with yourself, your life's activities, and your ministry achievements. Or it may show itself in your thrusting yourself forward before others into the spiritual spot-light at every opportunity, by always being the first to speak or volunteer to be in front of your peers in some way, for "ministry" of course. Even worse, it may demonstrate itself by you just ignoring your elder-teachers and mentors, failing to understand the great value they are to you as examples and guides for your future ministry.

The wisdom of Scripture is summed up in two words in this regard—slow down! You must be patient about attaining to leadership. In due time, you will have the opportunity to carry that burden, and be assured, it is a burden for which you will need great grace from God.

Paul warned in 1 Timothy 3:6 (i.e., in one of his lists of qualifications for spiritual and ministry leadership) that immature, inexperienced ministry trainees must not assume leadership too early, or it may destroy them. He wisely wrote concerning those who are to be appointed to church leadership over their fellow Christians, "And not a new convert, so that he will not become conceited and fall into the condemnation incurred by the devil." Paul chose the Greek term for "new convert," from which we get our English word "neophyte." A literal, more etymological translation of the term is "new plant," a tender, fragile shoot just growing up out of the ground, easily crushed under foot, or withered by a harsh environment. This refers to persons of limited experience and knowledge, over-inflated in their own opinion of themselves, and consequently naïve about what it really takes to be a leader of the people of God in the local church and among their peers in other Christian settings.

You may have been born again many years ago when much younger but being ready for leadership is not measured by how many years have passed since then, though the accumulation of experience as a Christian is important. You need the *abundant grace of God*, which will give you the ability to learn essential lessons about life and ministry, as Paul said in Titus 2:11–14: "For the grace of God has appeared bringing salvation to all men, instructing us to deny ungodliness and worldly desires and live sensibly, righteously and godly in the present age looking for the blessed hope and the appearing of the glory of our great God and Savior, Christ Jesus, who gave Himself for us to redeem us from every lawless deed, and to purify for Himself a people for His own possession, zealous for good deeds."

God, by His grace, instructs us in the essentials

of Christian experience, and that takes time. Of first importance in this instruction is that readiness for leadership is determined by the Body of Christ itself, in assessing your spiritual maturity, your giftedness from God, and your philosophy and experience in ministry. Being a humble servant of God who is a recipient of His grace is where the journey of ascendance to leadership among the people of God begins.

Questions for Reflection and Discussion

1. *Learning to follow Christ, which is growing in Christian maturity, is dependent upon knowing His strength and gaining His favor, the essential definition of what major bestowment from God to the believer?*

2. *For the Christian, what is the major prerequisite for receiving grace from God daily, beyond knowing God's saving grace?*

3. *How is humility best defined in the New Testament?*

4. *What does the New Testament say in James 4 and 1 Peter 5 about what God will do to the believer whose life is characterized by pride, the opposite of humility?*

5. *What are the two daily activities the disciple must do, according to James 4 and 1 Peter 5, to receive daily grace from God?*

6

Grace for Suffering

It wasn't long into my freshman year of university training, after I started my campus job and started slogging through all the assignments in each of my courses, that the suffering began. With meeting all my other daily responsibilities of attendance at chapel and other campus events, church services and outreach ministry, I began to feel weary physically, totally stressed out emotionally, and pretty hopeless spiritually.

I had never realized I was so weak in so many ways. But the "pressure cooker" for excellence wisely created by the university to train future Christian leaders revealed those weaknesses to me rather quickly. Then of course, from time to time like everybody, I got physically sick, which threw me behind in all my assignments and other responsibilities and created even more anxiety.

Though I was hungry for everything that was being served to me in my university experience, due to my own spiritual immaturity, weak character, and relatively undisciplined academic background, I suffered from fear every day and often a good measure of discouragement. Would I make it or would I fail on this test, this project, while presenting this next speech, or writing this next paper? That fear was rooted in my dread of being humiliated before others due to my inabilities, some imagined and some real. I was too proud to let anybody know my weaknesses and too proud to ask for help. This was not good. It made me an easy target for the Evil One.

Satan never missed an opportunity to oppose me.

He never let up, not ever. He tempted me. He accused me about my failures. He used my conscience against me. I wanted to be a holy, righteous man, to please the Lord in every possible way, so he saw to it that every time I faced even the smallest choice between right and wrong and failed, I was tortured by self-condemnation through my poorly educated conscience as a young Christian.

What was worse, I didn't have a grasp of what my Heavenly Father was really like. I loved Him and wanted to serve Him, but my perception of Him was all wrong, pathetically distorted, based on my own family experience with my dad, who was a strict disciplinarian and unrelenting taskmaster. Even though I knew my dad loved me and would sacrifice anything for me, he rarely showed it warmly, and he largely parented me through fear and severe punishment. He was one of the "Greatest Generation," a child of the Great Depression, who fought to deliver the world from fascist dictators during WWII and then came home to build a life of material prosperity. He succeeded. With his kids, whatever he said was the law and the slightest disobedience was met with harsh correction, both verbal and physical. I thought this was normal, and besides, it was always counterbalanced by my mother's happiness and tenderness.

Though I often feared my father, I always loved him. By the grace and mercy of God I never felt abused at all during those growing up years. I knew my father did love me, in spite of whatever deficien-

cies he had in showing that love. I am thankful the
Lord Jesus somehow gave me that knowledge as a
boy growing up. I am also grateful that as I grew
into adulthood and my father matured in the faith,
his warmth and kindness toward me grew. That was
a great kindness from God to me for which I am
profoundly grateful to this day.

But I didn't understand as a young Christian that
God as my Father was very different from my dad
during my upbringing, because I did not yet understand the Scriptures about Him. God is abundantly
"compassionate, and gracious, slow to anger, and
abounding in lovingkindness" (Psalm 103:8), a kind
father who understands all of our weaknesses and
is always ready to correct us, forgive us, and help us,
whatever our struggle. He will discipline us faithfully, but always wisely and just as much as we need,
no more and no less. As Psalm 103:13–14 puts it,
"Just as a father has compassion on his children, so
the Lord has compassion on those who fear Him.
For He himself knows our frame; He is mindful that
we are but dust."

In short, while my first four years at my Christian
college were the most exciting and gratifying years
of my life up to that point, they were also characterized by significant suffering, privately and regularly.
And what I didn't know and wish I had known, was
that God had an antidote for that suffering—*His
favor combined with His strength, His grace*, will-
ingly granted from the hand of a loving Heavenly
Father daily.

Suffering is a means God uses to make us holy, so we should never view it as a mindless evil born out of an impersonal fate, a destiny we cannot avoid in this broken world. We can literally come to the point in our Christian experience that we live what James wrote about suffering in James 1:2–8.

"Consider it all joy, my brethren, when you encounter various trials, knowing that the testing of your faith produces endurance. And let endurance have its perfect result, so that you may be perfect and complete, lacking in nothing. But if any of you lacks wisdom, let him ask of God, who gives to all generously and without reproach, and it will be given him. But he must ask in faith without any doubting, for the one who doubts is like the surf of the sea, driven and tossed by the wind. For that man ought not to expect that he will receive anything from the Lord, being a double-minded man, unstable in all his ways."

But how can this joy during many and varied trials ever be a reality in your life experience, I mean, *really*? Nobody *wants* to suffer, do they? Yet suffering is such an essential part of life, and yes, this side of Heaven, it is inevitable. There is a simple answer to finding this joy in suffering—*His grace, which is His favor combined with His strength*, imparted to you in the midst of the suffering. This is what the New Testament teaches.

Paul wrote about it especially as a result of his own experiences in suffering. At one point in his life, while he was serving Christ faithfully, God allowed suffering to come into his life in the form of a physical illness, an affliction caused by Satan himself. Satan's intent through the affliction was to destroy Paul and his ministry for Christ. God's intent was to keep him humble because of all the revelation He had given him, probably more than ever given to any other man, both in quality and quantity. Some of those revelations Paul wrote down, but others he was forbidden to record, according 2 Corinthians 12:4. After he prayed about his terrible physical illness three times, asking God to remove it, God made a vital lesson about grace clear to him. Paul wrote about this in 2 Corinthians 12:7–10.

"Because of the surpassing greatness of the revelations, for this reason, to keep me from exalting myself, there was given me a *thorn in the flesh* [italics added], a messenger of Satan, to torment me—to keep me from exalting myself! Concerning this I implored the Lord three times that it might leave me. And He has said to me, 'My grace is sufficient for you, for power is perfected in weakness.' Most gladly, therefore, I will rather boast about my weaknesses, so that the power of Christ may dwell in me. Therefore, I am well content with weaknesses, with insults, with distresses, with persecutions, with difficulties, for Christ's sake, for when I am weak, then I am strong."

In this passage, Paul brings up all kinds of suffering and he says Christ's grace is the answer for enduring in those sufferings and benefiting by them. This passage is central to understanding that one dimension of God's *grace* is His *strength* or *power*; it is not just an *attitude of undeserved favor* from God toward us, though it certainly is that as well.

As a young man, I remember thinking one day about Christian suffering and marveling that I had experienced so little of it, really—no extreme crises, no severe deprivations, no great losses, as I had read about and knew from firsthand experience other Christians faced. I wondered why I had experienced so little. But our Father knows what we need and can endure, . . . and when, for our good.

As life unfolded, year by year, they came, in the middle of family joy and fruitful ministry. They, unwelcome, intruded. Car accidents, broken limbs, surgeries, the loss of parents and a brother—all painful fires, burning away the dross.

Often, there seemed to be "too much month and not enough money" for a growing family, resulting in stress caused by "little faith" (Jesus's words) in such circumstances. This was another form of suffering brought on by my weakness.

There were years of unspoken grief over a prodigal son, who was long away before returning home and to Christ, a daily grief always standing nearby to darken light and steal joy. This was suffering. It was hard instruction in what I would never have chosen to know. It was learning what the grief-filled heart of our Father is toward us in our wanderings from Him. This was a kind of soul torture, yearning in daily prayer over a loved one enslaved by sin. This was joining the fraternity of a Broken-hearted Father, learning firsthand the fellowship of His sufferings over us when we like sheep dangerously wander away from Him. It was learning that in pain there can be joy, standing hand in hand with it, while serving Him in sorrow for those we love most.

Then came the sudden giving way of an ankle made weak by a lifetime of injuries, followed by reconstructive surgery, . . . resulting in permanent nerve damage. This was followed soon by illness, daily, then for months, unrelenting, followed by more surgery. Then, unexpected, a heart attack one day while driving back to the office after at lunch, followed by more surgery. Then, chronic illness, ever present, ever weakening, never leaving.

Following close behind these physical maladies, came "losses of the heart," not to be known by others. All men have them. They are ours to bear alone, only for God to know. And the astounding, great good of all this ? The beautiful mercy of every blow? The deep, settling joy from it? It showed me the bottomless depths of my insufficiency, my inadequacy, my inability, my weakness, . . . and continues to show me every day. It has shown me that all I need to see when I look into the dark pool that is my own heart is His shining face. He alone will sustain us, He will light the way. He, above all others, will hold us up. He favors the lowly and strengthens the weak. In His own words: "My grace is sufficient for you, for power is perfected in weakness" (2 Corinthians 12:7). He is the God of all grace, a grace free and abundant for all who believe. As Peter wrote,

"After you have suffered for a little while, the God of all grace, who called you to His eternal glory in Christ, will Himself perfect, confirm, strengthen and establish you. To Him be dominion forever and ever. Amen" (1 Peter 5:10).

So, when the pressure is on, the trouble starts, your health is failing, the temptations are flying at you from the right and the left, Satan is on the attack at every turn, and the light of hope is first dim and then extinguished, cry out to Him *for grace, for power.* He will give it to you. He *will* give it to you!

Questions for Reflection and Discussion

1. *In daily life, suffering often takes the form of a perceived lack of what we need, resulting in what internal reactions in the heart of a believer?*

2. *According to James 1, which counter-intuitive reaction to suffering is a daily possibility for the follower of Christ?*

3. *In Paul's experience of suffering, what was a positive outcome in his character though he had received unprecedented revelations from God potentially resulting in self-exaltation?*

4. *Who was the instrument God used to bring physical suffering to Paul, to help him remain humble as a servant of God?*

5. *In every form of suffering he experienced in service for Christ, Paul learned what vital lesson about grace from God?*

7

Grace to Serve

As the years of undergraduate training passed, I found myself better able to handle the workload, organize my life, and meet my other daily obligations as a student training for the ministry. However, most of my experiences in ministry on the weekends confronted me with a strange feeling of inadequacy, only to be met with the surprise of success in the form of at least some spiritual fruit as I served.

But still, in spite of that small measure of ministry fruitfulness, whenever I would prepare to go witness, preach, or serve Christ somewhere in some other way, I could never shake a strange and unwelcome sense of foreboding. What if no one would listen as I presented the gospel? What if I couldn't keep my thoughts and words in order while I preached, resulting in a shameful display of ministerial inadequacy? How embarrassing that would be! What if I gave a person seeking help from the Word of God the wrong advice? That could end in tragedy. The closer I got to graduation, the more overwhelming the knowledge became to me, that I was not ready for full-time, vocational Christian ministry. Remember, I had only been a Christian for five years and the inadequacy of my knowledge of Scripture and my lack of practical ministry skill and experience left me dreading the idea of pursuing a full-time ministry position of any kind.

I found what I thought was a simple solution for this problem—seminary. There, I could gain greater knowledge and give myself more time to accumulate the needed ministry experience and confidence I lacked. But deep down, I knew there was something else wrong. I just felt so weak spiritually, so lacking in faith, so full of fear. I knew I could never embark on a lifetime of ministry in this state of heart and mind, but I really didn't know the remedy for this serious problem.

While completing a graduate degree and entering into a ministry of teaching the Word and preaching at the Christian university where I had trained, more light came from God concerning what I needed in order to be stronger, more full of faith, and less fearful about the outcome of my service for Christ. Finally, in the crucible of being a new husband, a new father, a new teacher, a new PhD candidate and a new bi-vocational pastor, God opened my eyes to His great truth found in the Word of God about *grace for service*. This truth had been in the Scriptures all along, of course, but I just somehow had been mostly blind to it, until He who opened the eyes of the blind and gave me spiritual sight to see.

In Spite of Spiritual and Physical Inadequacy

I remember being confronted with Paul's assessment of himself as a servant of God. The great, indefatigable apostle, writer of epistles and empire-wide missionary-evangelist, wrote about himself in 2 Corinthians 3:4–6, "Such confidence we have through Christ toward God. Not that we are adequate in ourselves to consider anything as coming from ourselves, but our adequacy is from God, who also made us adequate as servants of a new covenant, not of the letter but of the Spirit; for the letter kills, but the Spirit gives life."

Even Paul knew what it was to feel inadequate in service for the advancement of the kingdom of God. He had also found a solution for another dimension of his own inadequacy—his physical frailty. He wrote, "But we have this treasure in earthen vessels, so that the surpassing greatness of the power will be of God and not from ourselves" (2 Cor 4:7).

Through the Impartation
of Grace by the Spirit

Later, in 2 Corinthians 9:8, Paul penned one of his remarkably summative comments, as he often does in his letters. This one captures his basis for confidence in spiritual life and ministry. His was a *grace-based confidence*, as he hoped would be the confidence of all believers after him. "And God is able to make all grace abound to you, so that always having all sufficiency in everything, you may have an abundance for every good deed."

This statement by Paul was part of his exhortation to the Corinthians concerning their monetary giving to the poor. But he stated it under inspiration in a way that makes the essential nature and sweeping promise of grace applicable in every area of spiritual life and ministry. The way he heaps up terms like "able," "all," "abound," "sufficiency," "everything," and "always" in this single statement about grace leaves the reader over-awed by this promise. Using the language of strengthening and empowerment, Paul often reasserted the truth of this passage in other letters he wrote. For example, to the Ephesian believers he wrote that he prayed for them,

"That he would grant you, according to the riches of His glory, to be strengthened with power through His Spirit in the inner man. So that Christ may dwell in your hearts through faith; and that you, being rooted and grounded in love, may be able to comprehend with all the saints what is the breadth and length and height and depth, and to know the love of Christ which surpasses knowledge, that you may be filled up to all the fullness of God. Now to Him who is able to do far more abundantly beyond all that we ask or think, according to the power that works within us, to Him be glory in the church and in Christ Jesus to all generations forever and ever. Amen" (Eph 3:16–21).

The Spirit's impartation of grace to the inner man achieves in a Christian far beyond even what that Christian can dare hope for or imagine possible—a sense of Christ's continual presence in his heart by faith, a grasp of the incomprehensible love of Christ by personal experience, and transformation into His full likeness, as much as is possible with the natural and sinful limitations of our humanity. All of this is by *His undeserved favor com-*

bined with His great strength—His grace. Writing to the Philippians, Paul instructs us, "For it is God who is at work in you, both to will and to work for His good pleasure" (2:13). We need never fear about having the desire and power to do God's will. He is at work in us by His grace all the time to achieve that end.

Remarkable Results of Grace

A life infused with the grace of God through Christ, imparted to the inner man by His Spirit, produces a level of spiritual fruitfulness not otherwise possible through normal human means. Abilities imparted through inherited traits, natural intelligence, strategic planning, and personal diligence may result in great works for the glory of God. But there is a level of spiritual achievement and productivity not attainable through these means alone. For men to be reached with the gospel, believers must be empowered by grace. For the Church to be built up, leaders and followers must be strengthened by grace. For eternal rewards to be won, Christians must be recipients of the grace of God to do the works necessary.

When grace is the power fueling a disciple's service for Christ, the outcome in that believer can be stunning, completely unexplainable in human terms. One man can accomplish more than many and appear to be a sort of giant standing on the landscape of Church history. This has been true of many men and women in the history of the church.

Believers today are still aware of the names Martin Luther, John Calvin, John Knox, John Bunyan, Jonathan Edwards, George Whitefield, William Carey, Mary Slessor, Adoniram Judson, Hudson Taylor, Amy Carmichael, Charles Spurgeon, D.L. Moody, Billy Sunday, and Bob Jones, Sr. This list could go on. Some of these Christians lived centuries ago, but they are still remembered because they modeled the *grace-filled life*.

This was certainly true of Paul, who is the prototypical example of the grace-filled servant of God. He explains how this occurred in his own case in his brief autobiography recorded in 1 Corinthians 15:9–10. "For I am the least of the apostles, and not fit to be called an apostle, because I persecuted the church of God. But by the grace of God I am what I am, and His grace toward me did not prove vain; but I labored even more than all of them, yet not I, but the grace of God with me."

Under inspiration, Paul is not demonstrating a false humility by calling himself "the least of the apostles" and "unfit to be called an apostle." This was his honest self-assessment, were it not for the saving and sanctifying grace of Christ in his life. That grace was also the explanation for his astounding ministry productivity. Essentially, he did more work for Christ than any other Christian of his generation, and understanding the language in this statement fully, perhaps more than all the others combined. This would be an offensively arrogant statement if it were not for what he credits this astounding level of fruitful service to—*the grace of God*. It made him what he was and empowered him to do what he did.

The fact of grace for service is like a rainbow of hope hanging over the future of every younger disciple who is anticipating a life of service to Christ, either as a leader in the church or simply as a faithful discile in the fellowship of believers. It dispels the darkness of inadequacy and fear, replacing it with the light of strength and faith. Your life can be like the seed of the Word sown on good ground, described by Jesus in the parable of the sower. You can produce a hundred times beyond yourself for His glory.

Christ even promised us that through His grace, imparted by His Spirit, we are actually able to perform greater works than He did during His incarnate ministry. This seems impossible because of who He is and His great power. If the words spoken by Him and recorded in John's Gospel were not written, this promise would be hard to believe. But considering the nature of His grace, the effect of His favor combined with His power through us, it is not at all impossible; in fact it is altogether possible. Jesus is God, working through us by His Spirit. All things are possible!

"Truly, truly, I say to you, he who believes in Me, the works that I do, he will do also; and greater works than these he will do; because I go to the Father" (John 14:12).

Questions for Reflection and Discussion

1. *What is a common negative experience of younger, more immature followers of Christ when they engage in acts of spiritual service?*

2. *According to Paul, what is the level of availability of the grace of God for service by believers for Christ?*

3. *According to Philippians 2:13, what will God by His grace produce in the heart of the believer with reference to service?*

4. *What spiritual exercise results in the Spirit's impartation of strength (grace) to the believer for service for Christ?*

5. *According to 1 Corinthians 15:10, what was the extent of Paul's productivity in ministry through the grace of God, which he described as being "with him"?*

8

Accessing the Grace of God Daily

I learned early on as a disciple that God is so gracious and so powerful that simply by virtue of who He is, we will be blessed as Christians, especially when compared to those who do not know Christ. But I also began to notice quite a disparity between *the favor and strength or grace* some Christians experienced compared to that of other Christians, who were weak and unproductive as followers of Christ. I later came to understand that having the grace of God abounding in one's own Christian experience finds its source in Christ; but like so many of the promises of God, it is dependent upon our desire, urgency, and determined pursuit of the means to acquire that grace presented to us in the New Testament. In other words, being grace-filled is not automatic simply because you are a Christian.

There are three principal means by which we may obtain an inflow of abundant grace from Christ into our hearts as believers. These are not unfamiliar ideas, but the fact that they are all directly connected to the reality of *experiencing God's grace* in your life may be new to you.

The Word of Grace

If you have been a believer long, you have heard your parents, pastor, and other teachers exhort you to read the Bible, listen to it, memorize it, meditate in it, study it, and obey it. The reason for this is simple. It is the Word of our God to you. It is your guide for your faith and daily practice as a follower of Jesus.

You have probably also heard lessons and sermons presenting the Bible as a mirror to reveal who you really are so that you can confess your sins, as water to drink spiritually and food to eat for your soul, which provides energy for your inner man, and as a lamp to guide you on the dark path of life in this world. These are all powerful images extolling the value of the Word of God to the believer.

But the New Testament gives another description of the Word of God to add to this list. It is the *Word of grace.* It is the means by which *the favor combined with the strength of God* is communicated to your soul daily. When Paul stopped briefly to speak to the Ephesian pastors on his journey back to Jerusalem after his third extensive missionary ministry, he made this truth clear to them. "And now I commend you to God and the word of His grace, which is able to build you up and to give you the inheritance among all those who are sanctified" (Acts 20:32).

The Word of God brings grace into the heart of believers to build them up in strength and prepare them for lives of service with and to other believers, both in this life and for eternity. We don't read the Bible just because we are obligated to do so. We read it because of the grace Christ provides for us through it daily.

The Fellowship of Grace

One of the other sources of grace for your heart is other believers. God uses other Christians to strengthen you with grace by what they say to you. Likewise, you do the same to other believers by what you say to them. This truth is taught in Ephesians 4:29: "Let no unwholesome word proceed from your mouth, but only such a word as is good for edification according to the need of the moment, so that it will give grace to those who hear."

This communication may be just in private conversation with another believer. This fact is why it is so important to control what we say to other Christians and how we say it. We will either be building them up by grace or tearing them down by harsh, unkind, impure, or just worthless communication.

Grace is also ministered to the Christian by other believers through the use of their gifts for teaching the Word of God or serving them in other ways. This is what Peter meant when he wrote 1 Peter 4:10–11 as mentioned earlier in this discussion: "As each one has received a special gift, employ it in serving one another as good stewards of the manifold grace of God. Whoever speaks is to do so as one who is speaking the utterances of God; whoever serves is to do so as one who is serving by the strength which God supplies; so that in all things God may be glorified through Jesus Christ, to whom belongs the glory and dominion forever and ever. Amen."

So, fellowship with other believers, informally or in a more organized way as a local church, is vital for you to receive the grace you need day by day as a servant of Christ. Again, fellowship with other Christians for worship, instruction, and mutual encouragement is not simply an obligation you face because it is commanded by God. You must have it, if you want to receive the grace you need.

The Throne of Grace

I know of no other single Christian responsibility grieved over more by pastor-teachers, evangelists, leaders, and full-time Christian workers than prayer. Their comments are always the same. "I don't pray enough." "The people of God have failed in the ministry of prayer." "No wonder we don't see revival, we don't pray for it." If these dedicated servants of Christ bemoan the prayerlessness of themselves and the church, how would they react if they knew the extent of *your* prayer experience daily?

Since prayer is the believer's principal means of communing with God, expressing adoration to Him and expressing faith in Him, prayerlessness in a Christian is an extremely serious problem; it is an egregious sin. It isn't a simple deficiency. It is a gross failure, a grave offense to God, and it insures weakness in the believer's life. God's sapphire throne in Heaven (yes, that is its color according to Ezekiel 1) has a name. It is called "the throne of grace." The fact that it is called this is highly suggestive, raising the acquisition of grace there to a level of supreme importance. Consider the exhortation of the writer to the Hebrews in 4:16, "Let us therefore draw near with confidence to the throne of grace, so that we may receive mercy and find grace to help in time of need."

It is in prayer at the throne of grace that believers find mercy for their own sins, compassion for others, and the grace they need to walk with God and bear fruit, day by day. The Bible is clear. Where there is much prayer there will be much spiritual grace, which is power. Where there is little prayer, there will be little grace. Where there is no prayer there will be no grace. If we want grace, the power of God, at work in our heart and through our ministries as disciples, we have to ask for it in prayer. And when we do, God will give it to us, generously, as our kind and loving Father.

Questions for Reflection and Discussion

1. *Why are some believers strong and productive as disciples, while others are not?*

2. *How many principal means of grace are there for believers given in the Bible?*

3. *What is the secret to accessing grace through the Scriptures, which are called the word of grace in Acts 20:32?*

4. *What are the principal means of engaging in the fellowship of grace?*

5. *What is the name of the throne where Christ's sits as our High Priest, listening to our prayers daily?*

9

Conclusion: A Right Perspective about Grace

After reading the New Testament for a while as a Christian, I noticed a pattern in Paul's letters. But it wasn't until I intentionally sat down and turned to the prayer (invocation) at the beginning of each of his letters and the prayer (benediction) at the end of each of them that I realized an important truth and was fully impacted by it. Paul prayed for grace in every instance for the believers he was writing to at the beginning and the end of each of his epistles. The term translated grace in these prayers (*charis*) occurs 156 times in the New Testament—it is a dominant idea, and not just in Paul's letters.

Grace is central to our salvation, our growth as Christians, our capacity to learn as we should, our capacity to suffer with a positive outcome, and our ability to serve faithfully and fruitfully.

Without grace, we will always wonder about God's attitude toward us and struggle along in weakness on the narrow way, even though we are His children and He is always faithful to us in His love and compassion. If we think of grace as living free of the guilt from the condemnation of the law of God, we think of it in only one of its dimensions. If we misunderstand grace as being an unbiblical freedom from the responsibility to show our love for God and others by obedience to God's commands, we'll never experience the favor, strength, and consequent joy only a right understanding of grace can bring. With grace, we will have *the sense of Christ's favor combined with the strength of Christ* we need every day as disciples of Him.

It is not surprising that the New Testament, with its thousands of words and profound instructions for Christian living ends with these words in Revelation 22:21, "The grace of the Lord Jesus be with you all. Amen."

So, ". . . let us have grace, by which we may offer to God an acceptable service with reverence and awe . . . ." (Heb 12:28). "Be strong in the grace that is in Christ Jesus" (2 Tim 2:1).

Answer Key
for Reflection
and Discussion
Questions

1
A Right Starting Point

1. *What is a good place to begin in seeking to understand any major truth for Christian living?*

   ANSWER: Understanding the nature of God.

2. *Which is the idea most opposite the Biblical idea of grace?*

   ANSWER: Earning God's favor by good character or good works.

3. *Which member(s) of the Trinity is(are) described as characterized by grace?*

   ANSWER: All of them—the Father, the Son, and the Holy Spirit

4. *On the basis of whose work will the believer receive grace from God?*

   ANSWER: Christ's work, on the cross.

5. *How does the New Testament describe the amount of God's grace available to the Christian believer?*

   ANSWER: Available with no limits, abundant.

2
Saved by Grace

1. *What effect does a Christian in a family have on the other family members coming to know Christ's grace for salvation?*

   ANSWER: Others may or may not come to know Christ's grace for salvation through a Christian family member.

2. *What effect does disharmony in a family have on family members coming to know Christ's grace for salvation?*

   ANSWER: Members of the family may become Christians by grace in spite of relational disharmony in the family.

3. *What is a common name given to the grace of God resulting in salvation through Christ?*

   ANSWER: Saving grace.

4. *What is the essential response of a person to the good news of God's saving grace through Christ's death for sin on the cross and His resurrection for that person to be saved from sin and hell and receive the gift of eternal life?*

ANSWER: Faith in the gospel of the grace of God (Acts 20:24)

5. *What two great qualities of God are demonstrated by God through his saving grace?*

ANSWER: His favor and His strength.

3
Growth by Grace

1. *What compelling reality will lead a new Christian to give others the gospel of saving grace?*

   ANSWER: His own recent experience of the saving grace of Christ through the gospel.

2. *Having experienced saving grace, how much knowledge of the Bible must the new believer have to give the gospel of Christ to others?*

   ANSWER: He must know the facts of the gospel of saving grace, but his knowledge of the Scriptures may otherwise be fairly limited based on his lack of exposure to them.

3. *Though a new believer in Christ has experienced saving grace from sin and hell, what may still be true concerning his relationship to sin?*

   ANSWER: He may still have sinful habits, developed while a non-believer and will always possess an indwelling predisposition to sin until he goes to Heaven.

4. *In addition to the gifts of deliverance from hell and the gift of eternal life,*

what begins for a new believer at the moment of saving grace?

ANSWER: Daily deliverance from sinful attitudes and actions.

5. *Based on the teaching of the New Testament, what is one of the ways daily deliverance from sinful attitudes and actions is described?*

ANSWER: Growth in grace and in the knowledge of the Lord Jesus Christ (2 Peter 3:18).

4
Gifted by Grace

1. *What are the three great gifts given to the believer by God at the moment of saving grace through faith in the gospel of Christ, as discussed before this chapter in this book?*

   ANSWER: Forgiveness for sin, deliverance from hell, and the promise of eternal life.

2. *What is the additional blessing believers are granted at saving grace discussed in this chapter?*

   ANSWER: Gifts for service in the body of Christ, the Church.

3. *According to 1 Peter 4:10–11, what are the two major categories of gifts for service presented by the Apostle?*

   ANSWER: Gifts of communication (speaking) and gifts of action (ministry).

4. *What is the basis for the gifts of service for believers given by God?*

   ANSWER: The manifold (many faceted) grace of God imparted to the believer through the Holy Spirit's ministry.

5. *On the basis of gifts of grace for service given to each believer in the New Testament, which are the more important gifts in the body of Christ?*

ANSWER: All gifts are equally important to the health and growth of the body of Christ, the Church.

5
Grace for Learning

1. *Learning to follow Christ, which is growing in Christian maturity, is dependent upon knowing His strength and gaining His favor, the essential definition of what major bestowment from God to the believer?*

   ANSWER: Grace.

2. *For the Christian, what is the major prerequisite for receiving grace from God daily, beyond knowing God's saving grace?*

   ANSWER: Humility

3. *How is humility best defined in the New Testament?*

   ANSWER: Viewing yourself as undeservingly favored by God, grateful for whatever there is of good in you by the kindness of God, and rightly subordinated to others to serve them.

4. *What does the New Testament say in James 4 and 1 Peter 5 about what God will do to the believer whose life is characterized by pride, the opposite of humility?*

ANSWER: He will resist him by not imparting daily grace.

5. *What are the two daily activities of the disciple must do, according to James 4 and 1 Peter 5, to receive daily grace from God?*

    ANSWER: Submit to God and submit to the example and instruction of spiritual leaders.

6
Grace for Suffering

1. *In daily life, suffering often takes the form of a perceived lack of what we need resulting in what internal reactions in the heart of a believer?*

   ANSWER: A sense of uncomfortable pressure, anxiety, weakness, and inability.

2. *According to James 1, which counter-intuitive reaction to suffering is a daily possibility for the follower of Christ?*

   ANSWER: Joy, in the trials that bring physical and spiritual suffering.

3. *In Paul's experience of suffering, what was a positive outcome in his character though he had received unprecedented revelations from God potentially resulting in self-exaltation?*

   ANSWER: He remained humble before God.

4. *Who was the instrument God used to bring physical suffering to Paul, to help him remain humble as a servant of God?*

   ANSWER: Satan, who was permitted to afflict

Paul physically. Satan's motive was to stop Paul's ministry and destroy him. God's motive was to keep him humble for service.

5. *In every form of suffering he experienced in service for Christ, Paul learned what vital lesson about grace from God?*

ANSWER: That grace was God's strength for every weakness, His sufficient power to sustain him in every kind of trial.

7
Grace to Serve

1. *What is a common negative experience of younger, more immature followers of Christ when they engage in acts of spiritual service?*

   ANSWER: A sense of inadequacy and weakness.

2. *According to Paul, what is the level of availability of the grace of God for service by believers for Christ?*

   ANSWER: According to 2 Corinthians 9:8, it is always available in full measure.

3. *According to Philippians 2:13, what will God by His grace produce in the heart of the believer with reference to service?*

   ANSWER: A desire for it and the strength to perform it.

4. *What spiritual exercise results in the Spirit's impartation of strength (grace) to the believer for service for Christ?*

   ANSWER: Prayer for all believers, according to Ephesians 3:14–21.

5. *According to 1 Corinthians 15:10, what was the extent of Paul's productivity in ministry through the grace of God, which he described as being with him?*

ANSWER: He labored more abundantly than everyone else in service in the first century, perhaps more than all others combined.

8
Access to the Abundant Grace of God Daily

1. *Why are some believers strong and productive as disciples, while others are not?*

   ANSWER: Some take advantage of the biblical means of grace and others do not.

2. *How many principal means of grace are there for believers given in the Bible?*

   ANSWER: Three; the Word of grace, the fellowship of grace, and the throne of grace.

3. *What is the secret to accessing grace through the Scriptures, which are called the word of grace in Acts 20:32?*

   ANSWER: Letting it dwell in you richly (Colossians 3:16), through reading it, memorizing it, meditating on it, listening to it, studying it, and obeying it (all the activities with reference to the Word of God prescribed for believers in the Bible).

4. *What are the principal means of engaging in the fellowship of grace?*

   ANSWER: Helping other believers by communicating edifying words which give grace to them

(Ephesians 4:29) and building them up through the exercise of our gifts of grace for their good (1 Peter 4:10–11).

5. *What is the name of the throne where Christ's sits as our High Priest, listening to our prayers daily?*

ANSWER: The throne of grace, where we obtain mercy and find grace to help in time of need.

Scripture Index

CPSIA information can be obtained
at www.ICGtesting.com
Printed in the USA
BVHW081303160122
626048BV00002B/13